The Countries

Peru

Bob Italia
ABDO Publishing Company

visit us at
www.abdopub.com

Published by ABDO Publishing Company, 4940 Viking Drive, Edina, Minnesota 55435.
Copyright © 2002 by Abdo Consulting Group, Inc. International copyrights reserved in all countries. No part of this book may be reproduced in any form without written permission from the publisher.

Printed in the United States.

Photo Credits: Corbis
Contributing Editors: Tamara L. Britton, Kate A. Furlong
Book Design and Graphics: Neil Klinepier

Library of Congress Cataloging-in-Publication Data

Italia, Bob, 1955-
    Peru / Bob Italia.
        p. cm. -- (The countries)
    Includes index.
    Summary: An introduction to the history, geography, people, economy, transportation, mass communication, and social life and customs of Peru, the third-largest country in South America.
    ISBN 1-57765-756-X
        1. Peru--Juvenile literature. [1. Peru.] I. Title. II. Series.

F3408.5 .I83 2002
985-dc21

                                                      2001045853

Contents

¡Hola!

Hello from Peru! Peru is a large country in South America. About 27 million people live there. **Indigenous** peoples make up about half of Peru's population.

Some Peruvians live along the Pacific coast. Others live high in the Andes Mountains, or deep in the Amazon rain forest. Peru's varied land provides homes for many different plants and animals.

During its history, Peru has had mighty indigenous empires. But its people have also suffered through wars, **terrorism**, and a poor **economy**. Today, Peruvians are working to strengthen their country for the future.

Hola *from Peru!*

Fast Facts

OFFICIAL NAME: Republica del Peru (Republic of Peru)

CAPITAL: Lima

LAND
- Mountain Range: Andes Mountains
- Highest Peak: Nevado Huascarán 22,205 ft. (6,788 m)
- Major River: Amazon River

PEOPLE
- Population: 26,490,000 (2002 est.)
- Major Cities: Lima, Cuzco
- Official Languages: Spanish, Quechua, Aymará
- Religion: Roman Catholicism

GOVERNMENT
- Form: Constitutional republic
- Chief of State: President
- Legislature: Democratic Constituent Congress
- Flag: Three vertical bands of red, white, red with the coat of arms in the center.
- Nationhood: 1821

ECONOMY
- Agricultural Products: Bananas, coffee, cotton, potatoes, sugarcane
- Mining Products: Copper, iron ore, lead, petroleum, silver, zinc
- Manufactured Products: Fish meal, metals, sugar, textiles
- Money: New sol (100 céntimos = 1 new sol)

LIMA ★

Peruvian flag

Peruvian currency

Timeline

1430s	Incas begin building their empire
1524	Spaniards explore Peru
1532-1824	Spain controls Peru
1824	Peru gains independence
1980s	Peru suffers from terrorism and a weak economy
1990-2000	Alberto Fujimori rules Peru as a dictator
2001	President Alejandro Toledo takes office

Lake Titicaca

Peru's Past

People have lived in Peru for more than 13,000 years. Early Peruvians lived in caves. They hunted animals and gathered food from the land. They used tools made of stone and bone.

Peru's civilizations slowly became more advanced. The people learned to plant and harvest crops. They became skilled at weaving, making pottery, and working with metal. They also built large temples.

In the 1430s, an **indigenous** group called the Inca began building an empire. Soon, the Inca empire included about 16 million people. The Inca's advanced system of government ruled its people.

In 1524, Spaniard Francisco Pizarro (frahn-SEE-sko pee-ZAH-roh) explored Peru. Spain granted him permission to establish a colony there. In 1532, Pizarro captured the Incan emperor. This gave Spain control over Peru.

Francisco Pizarro battles Atahualpa, the last Incan emperor.

Spain ruled Peru for nearly 300 years. Then in 1820, Argentina's José de San Martín (ho-ZEY day sahn mar-TEEN) led troops into Peru. They tried to free Peru from Spain, but failed. Four years later, Venezuela's Simón Bolívar (see-MOHN bo-LEE-var) succeeded in liberating Peru.

After becoming independent, Peru faced many problems. It changed leaders often. It lost wars against Bolivia, Colombia, and Chile. More recently, Peru experienced high **inflation**. And a **terrorist** group called Shining Path attacked Peru's government.

In the 1990s, Peru became more stable. Its president, Alberto Fujimori (ahl-BEHR-toh foo-gee-MOR-ee), improved the **economy**. Under Fujimori's leadership, police arrested Peru's terrorists. But Fujimori ruled Peru as a **dictator**. He shut down the congress and rewrote the **constitution**.

Many people accused Fujimori and his government of being **corrupt**. So in 2000, Fujimori was forced to step down as president. In 2001, the Peruvians elected a new president, Alejandro Toledo (ahl-eh-HAHN-dro toh-LEH-doh).

Congress President Carlos Ferrero (left) places the presidential sash on Alejandro Toledo. Toledo is Peru's first indigenous president. He promised to remain true to his roots and aid the nation's many poor citizens.

Rugged Landscape

Peru is South America's third-largest country. Its vast land has three main regions. These regions are the Costa (COH-sta), the Sierra (see-EHR-ah), and the Montaña (mohn-TAHN-yah).

The Costa region is a narrow strip of land along Peru's west coast. This land is a desert plain. Rivers that flow through the desert create **oases**. These oases provide rich farmland.

The Sierra region runs down the center of Peru. This region includes the Andes Mountains. They have high peaks covered by glaciers. In some places, fast-moving rivers have carved deep canyons into the mountains.

The southern part of the Sierra region contains Lake Titicaca (tih-tih-KAH-kah). It forms part of the border between Peru and Bolivia. It is the world's highest **navigable** lake. This lake is sacred to the Inca.

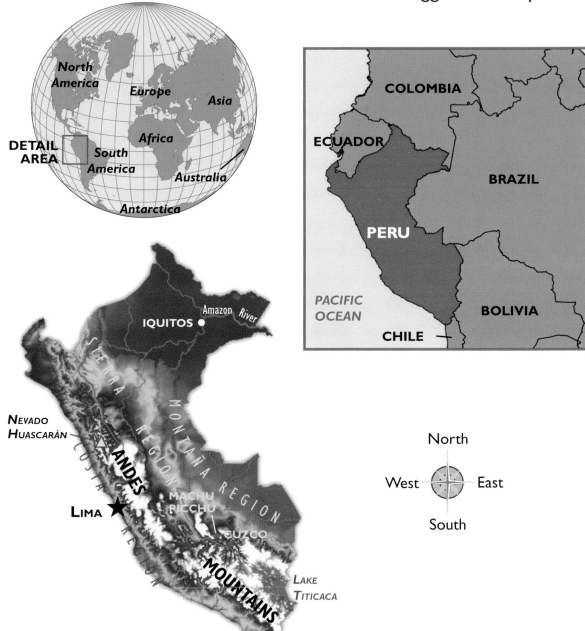

The Montaña region is in eastern Peru. Steep mountains, thick jungles, and sweeping plains are in this region. There are rivers, too. Some of them form the **headwaters** of the Amazon River. It is the second-longest river in the world.

Peru's climate varies from region to region. The Costa is normally dry with cool, foggy winters. The Sierra gets plenty of rain. It is warm at low elevations, and cool at high elevations. The Montaña is hot, sticky, and rainy.

Thick jungle covers the banks of this stream in the Montaña region.

Rainfall

AVERAGE YEARLY RAINFALL

Inches		Centimeters
Under 10		*Under 25*
10 - 20		*25 - 50*
20 - 40		*50 - 100*
40 - 80		*100 - 200*
Over 80		*Over 200*

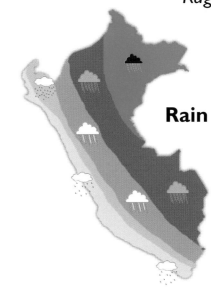

Rain

North
West — East
South

Temperature

AVERAGE TEMPERATURE

Summer

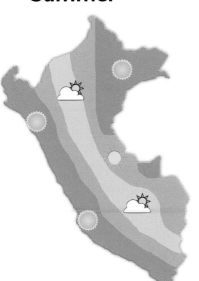

Fahrenheit		Celsius
65° - 80°		*18° - 27°*
50° - 65°		*10° - 18°*
32° - 50°		*0° - 10°*
Below 32°		*Below 0°*

Winter

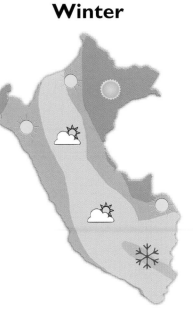

Plants & Animals

Each of Peru's regions has its own special plants and animals. In the Costa region, mesquite (muh-SKEET) trees and cacti grow well in the dry land. Pelicans, gulls, and sea lions live along the shore.

Grasslands, small shrubs, and trees cover the Sierra region. They are able to survive the region's cool nights and high winds. Animals such as llamas and vicuñas (vuh-COON-yahs) also live in this region. Their thick, woolly fur keeps them warm.

Grasslands in the Sierra region provide llamas with excellent grazing areas.

Rain forests and thick jungles cover the Montaña region. These areas are home to a wide variety of plants and animals. Some of these animals include jaguars, monkeys, and tapirs. Tapirs are hoofed mammals with long snouts.

A vicuña (above) and a tapir (below)

Peruvians

The Costa region is home to many **cultures**. Some Peruvians have Spanish roots. Their ancestors came to Peru when Spain controlled the area. Others are Italian, Chinese, Japanese, or African.

The Sierra region is home to many **indigenous** peoples. Most of these peoples live high in the Andes Mountains. They survive by farming. They are able to grow just enough crops to feed their families.

Indigenous peoples also live in the Montaña region. They live along the Amazon River or deep in the Amazon rain forest. The rain forest and its animals are sacred to many of these tribes.

Mestizos make up another part of Peru's population. Mestizos are people who are part indigenous and part European. Today, many Peruvians are mestizos. They live throughout the country.

Peruvians from the Sierra region gather to watch a local folk festival.

Several languages are spoken in Peru. Peru's official language is Spanish. Many of Peru's **indigenous** people speak Quechua (KEH-chuh-wah) or Aymará (i-muh-RAH). These are official languages in some parts of the country.

Peru's government grants its people freedom of religion. Nearly all Peruvians are Catholic. But many Peruvians blend the Catholic religion with indigenous beliefs.

Family is highly valued by most Peruvians. Social life in Peru often centers around family events. Family members often stay in contact with distant relatives.

Children in Peru must attend school from ages 6 through 15. But Peru's public schools have problems. Many schools are crowded. The teachers are not well trained. And the students lack good books and supplies.

Some students continue their education after age 15. They may go to a secondary school. Then some choose to attend one of Peru's 30 universities. Many study at San Marcos University in Lima. It opened in 1551, making it South America's oldest university.

Family events, such as weddings, are important in Peruvian society.

A family from the Montaña region stands in front of their home.

Each region in Peru has different types of homes. In the Costa region, many people live in tall apartment buildings. Homes of the Sierra region are made from **adobe** bricks, and have thatched roofs. In the Montaña region, people make their homes with wood and bamboo. They use grass to make the roofs.

Peruvians eat many different foods. They often enjoy corn and potatoes. These vegetables were important to Peru's **indigenous** peoples thousands of years ago.

Leche Asada

Leche asada is a sweet dessert enjoyed by people across Peru.

1 can sweetened condensed milk
1 cup sugar
8 eggs, beaten

1 can evaporated milk
1 tsp vanilla extract
1/4 cup water

Mix the condensed milk, evaporated milk, 1/2 cup sugar, vanilla, and eggs. Set aside. In a saucepan, mix water and remaining sugar. Heat until mixture forms a tan-colored syrup. Pour in a glass baking dish and cover with milk mixture.
Fill a large dish halfway with water. Place the glass baking dish in the dish of water. Cover with foil. Bake for 45 minutes at 400°F. Chill and serve cool.

AN IMPORTANT NOTE TO THE CHEF: Always have an adult help with the preparation and cooking of food. Never use kitchen utensils or appliances without adult permission and supervision.

LANGUAGE

English	Spanish	Quechua	Aymará
Yes _____	Sí _____	Ari _____	Jisa
No _____	No _____	Manan _____	Janiw
Thank You _____	Gracias _____	Yusulpayki _____	Yuspagara
Please _____	Por Favor _____	Allichu _____	Mirä ampi suma
Hello _____	Hola _____	Allillanchu _____	Kamisa(ra)ki
Goodbye _____	Adiós _____	Wuasleglla _____	Jakisiñkama
Mother _____	Madre _____	Mama_____	Tayka
Father _____	Padre _____	Tayta _____	Awki

Earning a Living

Many Peruvians work as farmers. Most farmers can only grow enough food to feed their families. A few farmers own huge farms and grow many crops. They export some of their crops to other countries. Peru's major crops are sugarcane, cotton, and coffee.

Mining is also important to Peru's **economy**. Peru's land is rich in minerals such as copper, silver, and iron. Peru's land also contains much **petroleum**. Workers mine petroleum from Peru's coast and rain forest.

In Peru's large cities, many people manufacture goods. Some people work in steel mills and shipyards. Other people work in factories that make chemicals, cement, paper, cars, or foods.

Farmers in the Sierra region separate wheat harvested on their farm.

Ancient Cities

Lima (LEE-muh) is Peru's capital and largest city. It is located near Peru's Pacific coast. Explorer Francisco Pizarro founded Lima in 1535. Since then, the city has served as the center of Peru's government, **culture**, and trade.

Iquitos (ee-KEY-tohs) is the largest city in Peru's Montaña region. It is a major port on the Amazon River. Thick jungle and steep mountains make traveling to Iquitos difficult. The only way in or out of the city is by boat or plane.

Cuzco (KOOS-koh) is a city high in the Andes Mountains. It served as the capital of the Incan empire. Today, modern buildings and ancient **ruins** stand side by side.

Machu Picchu (mah-choo PEE-choo) is an ancient Incan city northwest of Cuzco. The Inca abandoned this city hundreds of years ago. American Hiram Bingham discovered Machu Picchu in 1911. Today, tourists visit the city to see its **ruins** of temples, **plazas**, and homes.

Machu Picchu

From Here to There

Few Peruvians own cars. Many often travel by bus. Buses travel from place to place within large cities. They also carry passengers to nearby towns and villages.

Peru's major road is the Pan American Highway. It runs along Peru's west coast. The highway links Peru with Chile and Ecuador. Smaller roads connect Peru's villages and towns. Few of these roads are paved.

Unpaved roads, steep mountains, and thick jungles make driving across Peru difficult. Flying is an easier way to travel long distances within Peru. Twenty-four modern airports serve Peru's travelers.

Boats transport people along the Amazon River and its **tributaries**. People commonly use motorized canoes for short trips along the rivers. Large cargo boats carry people and goods longer distances. On Lake Titicaca, people often travel in reed canoes.

Reed canoes on Lake Titicaca

Republic of Peru

Peru is divided into 24 departments. The nation also has a **constitutional** province. Departments are similar to states in the United States. In 1987, the government began reorganizing the departments into regions. Today, this process is still underway.

Peru is a **republic**. Its people elect a president to govern the republic. The president serves a five-year term. After serving one term, a president can seek re-election.

Peru's president appoints a **cabinet** called the Council of Ministers. It helps the president govern the country. Two vice presidents and a **premier** also aid the president.

The Democratic Constituent Congress makes Peru's laws. The people elect the members of congress. Members of the congress serve five-year terms.

Peru's congress meets in July 2001 to swear in 120 new members.

Celebrations

When early Spanish **missionaries** came to Peru, they wanted to end the **indigenous** people's festivals. So they began celebrating Catholic saints' days with indigenous festivals.

Today, many of Peru's festivals are a mix of both Catholic and indigenous beliefs. Nearly every village has its own **patron saint**. Villagers celebrate their patron saint's day with dancing, music, food, and costumes.

In Cuzco, people celebrate the Incan festival Inti Raymi on June 24. It is Peru's shortest day of the year. People light fires to the sun god to bring back the light. They also dance, listen to music, and hold a ceremony.

Before the Inti Raymi ceremony, a man is chosen as the emperor of the Inca. He is carried to the ceremony on a platform. During the ceremony, dancers re-create an ancient battle for the emperor and the crowd.

The emperor is carried to the Inti Raymi ceremony.

Peruvians celebrate their independence on July 28 and 29. Many people do not have to go to work or school on these days. They watch parades and military displays. They also listen to Peruvian music.

Peruvian Culture

Peru's colorful **culture** provides many ways for people to have fun. Some people enjoy reading books by Peruvian authors. Watching sports is another popular activity. Many people also enjoy listening to music.

An ancient form of music from the Andes Mountains is called *música folklórica* (MOO-see-kah folk-LOHR-ee-kah). People play this music on flutes, panpipes, drums, rattles, and small guitars. People often play *música folklórica* at festivals.

Music from Peru's coast is much different. It is called *música criolla* (MOO-see-kah cree-OY-ah). This music blends Spanish and African rhythms. People play *música criolla* on guitars and wooden boxes. Many Peruvians enjoy dancing to this music.

Peruvians listen to modern music as well. Pop, rock, and jazz are popular in Peru. They also enjoy listening to other kinds of music such as salsa, cumbia, and chicha.

A band plays panpipes and drums at the **Plaza de Armas** *in Cuzco.*

Mario Vargas Llosa

Many Peruvians also enjoy reading books. One of Peru's most famous authors is Mario Vargas Llosa (mah-REE-oh VAHR-gahs YO-sah). In 1990, he ran for president of Peru, but lost to Alberto Fujimori. His novels explore Peru's **culture** and politics.

Watching soccer matches is another activity many Peruvians enjoy. The soccer season lasts from March to November. During that time, many Peruvians attend matches at Lima's national stadium.

Bullfighting also draws large crowds. They watch a person called a matador fight a bull. The matador swings a cape to get the bull to charge him. When the bull gets close, the matador tries to kill it with a sword.

Many Peruvians still enjoy making traditional crafts. They use ancient weaving methods to make ponchos, belts, and rugs. People still make pottery based on ancient designs, too. Today, these items are popular with Peru's many tourists.

A woman weaves traditional Peruvian cloth.

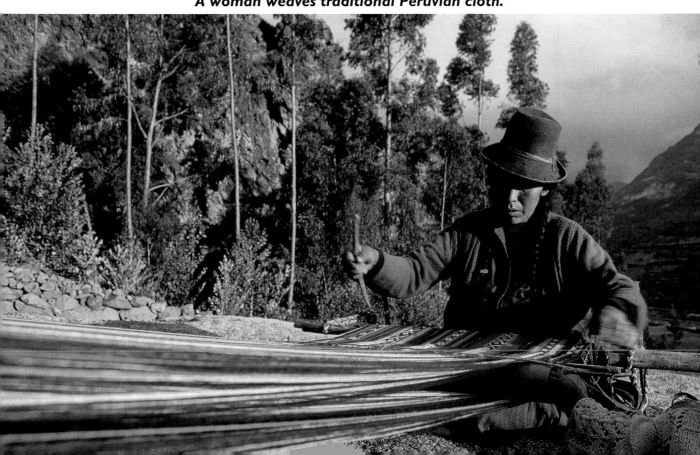

Glossary

adobe - a brick or building material of sun-dried earth and straw.

cabinet - a group of advisers chosen by the president to lead government departments.

constitution - the laws that govern a country.

corrupt - to be influenced by other people to be dishonest.

culture - the customs, arts, and tools of a nation or people at a certain time.

dictator - a ruler who has complete control and usually governs in a cruel or unfair way.

economy - the way a nation uses its money, goods, and natural resources.

headwaters - small streams that join to form a large river.

indigenous - native.

inflation - a rise in the price of goods and services.

missionary - a person who spreads a church's religion.

navigable - able to be sailed on by boats or ships.

oases - places in the desert with water, trees, and plants.

patron saint - a saint believed to be the special protector of a church, city, state, or country.

petroleum - a thick, yellowish-black oil. It is the source of gasoline.

plaza - a public square or open space in a community.

premier - the highest-ranked member of a government, also called a prime minister.

republic - a form of government in which authority rests with voting citizens and is carried out by elected officials such as a parliament.

ruins - the remains of something that has been destroyed.

terrorism - the use of terror, violence, or threats to frighten people into action.

tributary - a river or stream that flows into a larger stream, river, or lake.

Web Sites

Conquistadors – Peru
http://www.pbs.org/opb/conquistadors/peru/peru.htm
This site from PBS has a wealth of information on the Inca Empire and Francisco Pizarro's journey. Visitors can also view a timeline of Spanish conquests in the New World and learn how they have affected life there today.

Embassy of Peru
http://www.peruemb.org/main.html
This site from Peru's embassy in Washington, D.C., has information on Peru's geography, people, and economy. This site is also preparing to open a children's section soon.

These sites are subject to change. Go to your favorite search engine and type in Peru for more sites.

Index